JBIOG
Mary
Buchanan, Jane.

Mary Tudor: courageous queen
or Bloody Mary?

*Before her never was read in
story of any King or Queen of
England . . . under whom in
time of peace, by hanging,
beheading, burning, and
prisoning, so much Christian
blood, so many Englishmen's lives,
were spilled within this realm,
as under the said Queen Mary.*

John Foxe, a historian of
Christian martyrs, 1583

This book is for Sally.

Photographs © 2008: akg-Images, London: 71 top (Matthäus Merian), 33 (Ferdinand Pauwels); Alamy Images: 61 (Classic Image), 10 (Mary Evans Picture Library), 35, 70 bottom (John Morris); Art Resource, NY: 73 bottom (Alinari/Museo Nazionale di Capodimonte, Naples, Italy), 72 bottom (Bildarchiv Preussischer Kulturbesitz), 75 top, 98 (Guildhall Art Gallery, London, Great Britain/HIP), 74 top, 109 (Erich Lessing/Museo del Prado, Madrid, Spain), 17, 70 top right (Erich Lessing/Portraitgalerie, Schloss Ambras, Innsbruck, Austria), 25 (Victoria and Albert Museum, London, Great Britain); Bridgeman Art Library International Ltd., London/New York: 68 (Giovanni Battista Cipriani/Victoria & Albert Museum, London, UK), 73 top, 79 (Frank Cadogan Cowper/Palace of Westminster, London, UK), 89 (George Cruikshank/Private Collection), 73 center (Hippolyte Delaroche/National Gallery, London, UK), 52 left, 71 center (Sarah Countess of Essex/Private Collection/The Stapleton Collection), 20, 72 center (Fitzwilliam Museum, University of Cambridge, UK), 105 (Giraudon/Musee Conde, Chantilly, France), 43 (William Hogarth/Private Collection), 18, 70 top left (Hans the Younger Holbein/Walker Art Gallery, National Museums Liverpool), 75 bottom, 117 (National Portrait Gallery, London, UK), 113 (Francois Edouard Picot/Chateau de Versailles, France), 102 (Private Collection), 95 (Trustees of the Bedford Estate, Woburn Abbey, UK), 72 top (George Vertue/Private Collection); Corbis Images: 28 (Bettmann), 52 right (Hans the Younger Holbein/The Gallery Collection), 50 (Hulton-Deutsch Collection), 74 center (Martin Jones); Getty Images/Mansell: 120; Mary Evans Picture Library: 55, 56; The Granger Collection, New York: 74 bottom; Wellcome Library, London: 66, 71 bottom.

Illustrations by XNR Productions, Inc.: 4, 5, 8, 9
Cover art, page 8 inset by Mark Summers
Chapter art for introduction and chapters 9, 11, 12 by Roland Sarkany
Chapter art for chapters 1, 2, 3, 4, 5, 6, 7, 8, 10, 13, 14, 15, 16, 17, 18 by Raphael Montoliu

Library of Congress Cataloging-in-Publication Data

Buchanan, Jane, 1956-
Mary Tudor : courageous queen or Bloody Mary? / Jane Buchanan.
p. cm. — (A wicked history)
Includes bibliographical references and index.
ISBN 13: 978-0-531-12595-3 (lib. bdg.) 978-0-531-20502-0 (pbk.)
ISBN 10: 0-531-12595-5 (lib. bdg.) 0-531-20502-9 (pbk.)
1. Mary I, Queen of England, 1516-1558—Juvenile literature. 2. Great
Britain—History—Mary I, 1553-1558—Juvenile literature. 3.
Queens—Great Britain—Biography—Juvenile literature. I. Title.
DA347.B83 2008
942.05'4092—dc22
[B]
2007037487

Tod Olson, Series Editor
Marie O'Neill, Art Director
Allicette Torres, Cover Design
SimonSays Design!, Book Design and Production

© 2008 Scholastic Inc.

1 2 3 4 5 6 7 8 9 10 R 17 16 15 14 13 12 11 10 09 08   23

A WICKED HISTORY™

Mary Tudor

Courageous Queen
or Bloody Mary?

JANE BUCHANAN

Franklin Watts
An Imprint of Scholastic Inc.
New York   Toronto   London   Auckland   Sydney
Mexico City   New Delhi   Hong Kong
Danbury, Connecticut

The World of Mary Tudor

After fighting off opposition, Mary Tudor became
the first queen to rule England.

Irish
Sea

ENGLAND

NORF(
E

Ludlow Castle
B

WALES

SUFF

HERTFORDSHIRE

ESSEX

C Hatfield

A

Windsor • London

Bristol Channel

KENT **D**

Winchester **G**

F

DEVON
D

CORNWALL
D

English Channel

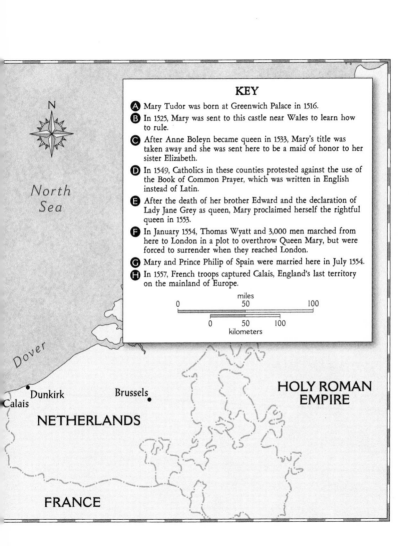

KEY

A Mary Tudor was born at Greenwich Palace in 1516.

B In 1525, Mary was sent to this castle near Wales to learn how to rule.

C After Anne Boleyn became queen in 1533, Mary's title was taken away and she was sent here to be a maid of honor to her sister Elizabeth.

D In 1549, Catholics in these counties protested against the use of the Book of Common Prayer, which was written in English instead of Latin.

E After the death of her brother Edward and the declaration of Lady Jane Grey as queen, Mary proclaimed herself the rightful queen in 1553.

F In January 1554, Thomas Wyatt and 3,000 men marched from here to London in a plot to overthrow Queen Mary, but were forced to surrender when they reached London.

G Mary and Prince Philip of Spain were married here in July 1554.

H In 1557, French troops captured Calais, England's last territory on the mainland of Europe.

North
Sea

N

miles
0   50   100

0   50   100
kilometers

Dover

Calais
Dunkirk
Brussels

NETHERLANDS

HOLY ROMAN EMPIRE

FRANCE

TABLE OF CONTENTS

A Wicked Web

A look at the allies and enemies of Mary Tudor.

The Family

HENRY VIII
Mary's father

CATHERINE OF ARAGON
Mary's mother; first wife of Henry VIII (divorced)

ANNE BOLEYN
second wife of Henry VIII (beheaded)

ELIZABETH
daughter of Anne Boleyn and Henry VIII; Mary's half sister

JANE SEYMOUR
third wife of Henry VIII (died)

EDWARD VI
son of Jane Seymour and Henry VIII; Mary's half brother

ANNE OF CLEVES
fourth wife of Henry VIII (divorced)

MARY TUDOR, QUEEN OF ENGLAND

CATHERINE HOWARD
fifth wife of Henry VIII (beheaded)

CATHERINE PARR
sixth wife of Henry VIII (outlived Henry VIII)

Mary's Catholic Allies

CHARLES V
King of Spain and head of the
Holy Roman Empire

PHILIP II
son of Charles V; became
Mary's husband

EUSTACE CHAPUYS
ambassador to England from
Charles V

SIMON RENARD
ambassador to England from
Charles V

Mary's Protestant Adversaries

THOMAS CRANMER
archbishop of Canterbury

DUKE OF
NORTHUMBERLAND
head of the council that advised
young King Edward

JANE GREY
grandniece of Henry VIII;
Northumberland's daughter-in-law

THOMAS WYATT
plotted to overthrow Mary and
put Elizabeth on the throne

HENRY DUDLEY
also plotted to
overthrow Mary

MARY TUDOR, 1516–1558

IN FEBRUARY THE BURNINGS BEGAN.

Guards woke the preacher John Rogers in his prison cell on the fourth day of the month. It was time, they said.

Rogers had slept well the night before. He was calm and smiling as the guards led him through the streets of Smithfield. He knew he was about to die. But he felt certain his death would carry God's true message to the people.

Since 1535, Rogers had preached the new Protestant faith. He gave his church members a Bible in English and told them to get rid of their old Latin version. He spoke out against the Roman Catholic Church and the Pope. He was a priest, yet unlike Catholic priests, he was married and proud of it. All of these things had gradually become legal in England over the last 20 years.

Now, the country had a new queen. Her name was Mary Tudor, and in her view, Protestants like Rogers were heretics. They angered God by rejecting the teachings of the Catholic Church. Their actions placed all of England in danger, Mary believed. She could not in good conscience stand for it.

In December 1554, Mary got the English Parliament to agree with her. They passed a law allowing her to burn heretics at the stake. Already she had begun to put her signature on the death warrants. John Rogers's was the first.

As Rogers approached the stake, he passed his wife and 11 children. He had not been allowed to say a private goodbye. Now he smiled at them and spoke a few words. Guards had to hold his family back while he was led away.

Rogers was one of the lucky ones. He died quickly. The wood caught fire at once and burned fiercely. After he was gone, a flock of doves circled overhead. Protestants who watched the burning said the doves had come to carry Rogers's soul to heaven.

Queen Mary did not witness the burning. And she did not believe that Rogers deserved to rest in heaven. Rogers and the others had chosen "to deceive simple persons," she insisted. They must be brought to justice. Their deaths would help teach others to avoid the "new and false opinions" of Protestantism. If England could be saved from heresy, she felt, a few deaths were a small price to pay.

Rogers, however, was only the beginning. The burnings would continue month after month for nearly three years. And Mary Tudor, the first reigning Queen of England, would be remembered for the next five centuries as Bloody Mary.

PART 1

The Princess Is a Pawn

CHAPTER 1

A Girl Child

Princess Mary is born and PROMISED IN MARRIAGE.

MARY TUDOR WAS BORN FEBRUARY 18, 1516. That she was a girl was disappointing to her parents. But at least she survived.

Mary was the fifth child born to King Henry VIII of England and his Spanish queen, Catherine of Aragon. The first four, two of whom were sons, had died at birth or soon after. The king badly needed a son to take the throne when he died. A daughter would not do. No woman had ever ruled England before.

MARY WAS THE FIRST SURVIVING CHILD of King Henry
VIII and Queen Catherine (above). Catherine had given birth to
four children who had not survived.

For now, however, Mary was the only heir. And
Henry made sure she was treated like a princess.
Dozens of ladies waited on baby Mary. Four women
were employed to rock her when she needed comfort.
She had other attendants to dress her and feed her.
All the while, she was surrounded with jewels and
furs and other luxuries. When Mary was old enough,
she sat on a tiny throne made of gold and velvet.

Mary did not see her parents often. She lived in a different part of the castle from the king and queen. But she was adored by her mother. And her tall, commanding father seemed to soften when he saw his daughter. He called her the "Pearl of the Kingdom."

KING HENRY VIII DOTED on his daughter Mary. But he was still desperate for a male heir.

Before long, Henry was ready to present his pearl to the world. It was time to find Mary a husband. Like most royal children, the princess was not expected to choose her partner. She would marry for the good of the kingdom, not for love.

In Henry's view, that meant that Mary's husband should come from France. The French king, Francis I, agreed and offered his son, Prince Francis. Both rulers were tired of fighting costly wars with each other. A marriage between the two royal families would help to bring peace.

And so Greenwich Palace prepared to celebrate Mary's engagement to the French prince. Hundreds of French visitors arrived at the castle, just outside of London. They paraded through the streets on horseback. Their fancy clothing drew gasps from the English crowd. At the castle, parties and feasting kept the fires in the kitchen hot for days.

Finally, Mary was ready to perform her first duty to England. She appeared for the ceremony in a

POWER PLAY

IN THE EARLY 1500s, ENGLAND WAS ONE OF Europe's three great powers. France was another. And the Holy Roman Empire was the third.

England's Henry VIII was an energetic and powerful king. But because of his country's small size, Henry needed one of the bigger powers as an ally.

In 1519, the King of Spain was elected Holy Roman Emperor. Charles V now ruled almost half of Europe.

Charles was a powerful man. He was also Queen Catherine's nephew. Henry certainly did not want him as an enemy. But he wanted to keep France as an ally, too. So his friendships with the two powers were always shifting.

As a child, Mary knew little about her father's political games. But those games had already come to rule her life.

CHARLES V CONTROLLED almost half of Europe.

golden dress. A velvet cap studded with jewels covered her blonde curls. Her mother stood just behind her. Her father stood before his throne near the Lord Admiral of France. The admiral was there to represent the prince, who had not made the trip.

Mary listened patiently to a long speech about the importance of marriage. Then the Lord Admiral approached her. He pushed a tiny ring with a large diamond onto Mary's finger. Mary sweetly offered to kiss the French nobleman. She thought he was her fiancé.

It was an understandable mistake. Mary was just two and a half years old. And she had never met the prince, who was barely one year old.

At the time of her engagement, Mary was just learning to talk. Yet she was already serving the purpose she was born for. She had made a match that would make her father a more powerful king.

CHAPTER 2

Education of a Princess

MARY IS TAUGHT to be an observant Catholic.

BY THE TIME OF MARY'S ENGAGEMENT, Queen Catherine was pregnant again. In the fall of 1518, she gave birth. And Henry's hopes for a son were dashed again. The child was a girl, and she did not survive. Disappointed, Henry blamed Catherine.

Mary, however, was more important than ever to the kingdom. Her many attendants watched her closely.

Her health was a constant concern—in England and in France.

The royal family moved around constantly. It was the king's duty to visit all parts of his kingdom. Henry kept 60 homes all across England for the purpose. There were castles in Windsor and Hanworth, in Richmond and Greenwich and London.

When the king moved into a castle, his entire court moved with him. Henry's court included 800 servants, advisers, friends, and family. In a few weeks, the castle was filthy. Horses and dogs had soiled the grounds. It was time to move on so the place could be cleaned and repaired.

Mary's own household took 26 carts to move. There were linens, furniture, and clothing to pack. Heavy woven tapestries went with her to decorate the walls. As they traveled, Mary's ladies all wore the official colors of the princess, blue and green.

One of the most important members of Mary's household was her teacher, a Spanish scholar named

Juan Luis Vives. Vives wrote a book specially for Mary called *The Education of a Christian Woman*. With guidance from Vives's book, Mary learned the skills she would need to be the wife of a powerful man. She was taught to speak several languages, including Spanish and Greek. Latin was a requirement, since it was the language of the Catholic Church. So was French, since that was the language of her fiancé.

If there was joy in Mary's life in those years, it came from music. Her favorite instrument was the lute, a guitar-like stringed instrument. She also played a keyboard instrument called the virginal. Music was a love she shared with her father, who played many instruments himself. He sometimes invited her to play with him to entertain guests. On those occasions she glowed like a pearl.

But if music gave her joy, religion gave her peace. With help from Vives, Mary was raised to be an observant Catholic. She prayed daily and went to Catholic Mass. She spent hours translating Bible

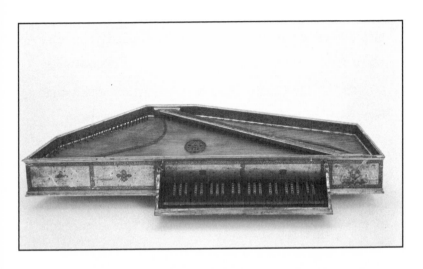

THIS VIRGINAL, A TYPE OF TINY PIANO, belonged to Mary's sister, Elizabeth. As a child, Mary often entertained guests along with her father, who was also a musician.

passages from Latin. Her education made it clear, however, that the true meaning of the words was not up to her to decide. Only the Pope, who ruled the Church from Rome, could interpret the word of God.

There was little room for fun in Mary's education. Her attendants did not allow men near her for fear she would learn to enjoy their company. Nor did she spend much time alone. Thinking, Vives wrote, was bad for a girl. She might be tempted by sinful thoughts. Instead, Mary read stories about women who sinned and were punished. They were meant to remind her what happened to girls who did not behave properly.

But while Mary learned to be an observant Catholic, a revolt was underway against the Pope and the priests who ran the church. It began 400 miles away in what is now Germany. It would eventually spread through Europe and beyond. In the process, it would change Mary's life—and the world—forever.

CHAPTER 3

Revolt!

Mary gets a new fiancé, while A RELIGIOUS REVOLUTION BREWS IN EUROPE.

Mary NEVER MET THE MAN WHO changed the direction of her life. He was a German monk named Martin Luther. And while Mary prayed and went to Mass, Luther attacked the church she was growing to love.

Martin Luther started his revolt in 1517, in Wittenberg, Germany, where he posted his famous "Ninety-five Theses" on the cathedral door. These were a list of complaints against the Catholic Church. Luther insisted that priests and the Pope were abusing their power. Under church rules, priests were allowed to promise worshippers that God would not punish them for their sins. The promise—called an indulgence—cost money. The Pope and other church officials, Luther charged, were getting rich on indulgences while peasants starved.

MARTIN LUTHER WAS A GERMAN MONK and a fierce critic of the Catholic Church. Henry VIII responded to Luther's criticisms of the church with a book accusing Luther of heresy.

Luther claimed that a person's relationship with God was personal. A priest had no right to intervene. The faithful did not need priests or the Pope in order to worship God, Luther declared.

With the help of a brand-new technology, people were beginning to listen. Luther used the recently invented printing press to publish copies of his Ninety-five Theses. Before long, his words spread throughout the Christian world, including England. The Protestant Reformation had begun.

The Reformation made a lot of people angry. The Holy Roman Emperor, Charles V, vowed to put an end to the revolt. Mary's father promised his support. King Henry called Luther a "weed" and an "evil-minded sheep." The Pope, Henry declared, was the supreme ruler of the church. Anyone in England who openly supported Luther would be arrested.

Mary was too young to understand what was happening. But once again, her life was swept up in events beyond her control. Henry's defense of the

Catholic Church strengthened his friendship with Charles V.

Meanwhile, Henry's brief alliance with France had broken down. He and Charles agreed to go to war against France. Any land or wealth won would be split between the two countries. To seal the deal, Henry promised Mary's hand in marriage to Charles.

That was the end of Mary's engagement to the French prince. At age six, Mary was now engaged to her 22-year-old Spanish cousin, Charles V.

Charles wanted Mary to come to Spain when she was seven. That way she could be trained properly to be a Spanish lady. Henry said no. She would stay in England until she was 12.

In 1522, guests again gathered at Greenwich Castle to celebrate the young girl's engagement. Charles came from Spain, and the celebrations lasted several weeks.

Over the following years, Mary wrote to her future husband regularly to declare her love. When she was nine, she sent him an emerald ring. She hoped he would stay faithful to her, she said, just as she was to him.

Shortly after Charles received the ring, however, he broke off the engagement. Like King Henry VIII, he needed an heir. He decided he couldn't wait for the young girl to grow up. He married another cousin, Princess Isabella of Portugal. But it was not the last Mary would hear from Charles.

BELIEFS TO DIE FOR

IN MARY'S TIME, THE PRIESTS AND THE POPE controlled their worshippers' relationships with God. They interpreted the Bible. They determined whether people's sins would be forgiven.

Martin Luther argued that people didn't need priests or the Pope. Worshippers had their own personal relationships with God.

Protestants also questioned many of the Catholic rituals. Luther's followers wanted all art depicting Bible stories removed from their churches. They felt the artwork led people to worship objects or "idols" rather than God.

Catholics and Protestants also disagreed about Holy Communion. During communion, worshippers share bread and wine. Catholics believed the bread and wine actually turned into Jesus' body and blood. Most Protestants considered the food to be a symbol—not real flesh and blood.

Why were these beliefs worth dying for? The faithful felt sure that believing the wrong thing could ruin a person's chance to live forever in heaven. It could also bring the anger of God down upon an entire country. That's why heresy became a matter of law—and offenders were often punished with death.

IN 1517, **MARTIN LUTHER NAILED** his Ninety-five Theses to a church door in Wittenberg, which was part of the Holy Roman Empire. This protest would change the course of history.

CHAPTER 4

Divorce

MARY COMES OF AGE with her family crumbling around her.

MARY HAD LITTLE TIME TO THINK ABOUT the loss of her second fiancé. In 1525, her father decided she should move close to Wales, a wild land to the west that had been ruled by English kings for two and a half centuries. Henry and Catherine still had not produced a son. If Mary was to inherit the throne, she needed to learn how to rule. As Princess of Wales, she would get her education.

Catherine was not happy about being separated from her daughter. But she had no choice in the matter. In August, Mary's attendants packed dozens of carts with her belongings. In all, 304 people traveled with her.

Mary moved into Ludlow Castle near Wales. Her ladies were under strict orders to keep her rooms clean and tidy. Mary was to have pleasant and cheerful conversation at all meals. She would continue her music studies and could dance on occasion.

WHEN MARY WAS NINE, she moved here, to Ludlow Castle near Wales. At the time, Wales was a small country under England's control.

Mary spent the next two years learning to be a princess. She traveled to all her father's properties in Wales. Wherever she went, people greeted her with respect and love.

By the time she returned to Greenwich Palace, Mary was 11. She was beginning to enjoy her role as princess. What she found at home must have come as a shock. Her parents' marriage was falling apart—and with it, Mary's chances of becoming queen.

Henry was still desperate to have a son, and he blamed Catherine for their failure to produce one. Catherine was too old to have another child. Henry was determined to divorce her and marry a younger woman. And he had just the woman in mind.

For a year now, the king had been secretly involved with a young woman from Catherine's court. Her name was Anne Boleyn, and Henry was quite in love with her. King Henry was determined to have Anne. And Anne was determined to be queen.

There was just one problem. Marriage in 16th-century Europe was controlled by the Catholic Church. To get a legal divorce, the king needed permission from the Pope. At first, Henry didn't see this as a big obstacle. Divorce was frowned upon. But it was not uncommon, especially among powerful people like the king of England.

Catherine, however, refused to give up her role as queen without a fight. When she heard of her husband's plans to divorce her, she sent a secret message to her nephew Emperor Charles V asking for help. Charles's armies, at this point, controlled Rome and the Pope. The emperor simply sent word to the Pope. And Henry was denied his divorce.

The king was furious. A battle between the princess's parents had begun. Mary, nearly a teenager now, lived with her own household, usually a few miles from the king's court. Still, she was caught in the middle of the royal feud.

Henry's ambassador to the Pope continued to push for the divorce. In the meantime, Anne moved into her own apartments in the royal castle. The stress took its toll on Mary. She suffered from stomach problems that made it difficult for her to eat.

In the summer of 1531, Henry grew tired of waiting. He told Catherine he never wanted to see her again. Then he ordered her to a palace 30 miles away in Hertfordshire. Mary was sent to Richmond Castle. Anne saw both women as rivals for the throne. Probably at her urging, Catherine and Mary were ordered not to see each other.

Anne, meanwhile, moved into Catherine's apartments at Greenwich Palace. Soon she was seen wearing Catherine's jewels. Henry began to take her to public events in place of the queen.

Then, in February 1533 came a shocking piece of news. Mary's father had not been able to get what he wanted from the Pope. So he declared that he would take action himself. He officially separated the Church of England from the Catholic Church in Rome. The Pope, Henry declared, no longer had authority over English worshippers. Instead, the king himself became the Supreme Head of the Church of England.

Henry gave the second-most-important title, archbishop of Canterbury, to his close ally Thomas Cranmer.

In April, messengers arrived at Richmond Castle. They told Mary that Archbishop Cranmer had declared her parents' marriage to be illegal. That meant that Mary was no longer a princess. What's more, the messengers told Mary, her father had married Anne Boleyn.

And that wasn't all. Mary's new stepmother was said to be pregnant.

PART 2

A Princess

in

Exile

CHAPTER 5

Queen Anne

Mary gets a WICKED STEPMOTHER.

AFTER THE DIVORCE, MARY STAYED AT Richmond. She waited nervously to see what would happen to her. Her mother still hoped that the Pope would fix everything. "In this world I will confess myself to be the king's true wife," Catherine wrote. "And in the next, they will know how unreasonably I am afflicted."

But events were moving quickly. In May 1533, Anne Boleyn was crowned queen. In September, she gave birth to a daughter named Elizabeth. Mary wrote a letter to her mother to comfort her. But soon, it was Mary who would need support.

AFTER DIVORCING MARY'S MOTHER, Catherine, Henry VIII married Anne Boleyn. Here, he presents the new queen to his court. Queen Anne soon gave birth to Elizabeth, who replaced Mary as heir to the throne.

That fall, Henry's advisers appeared at Mary's door with a warning. She was to stop calling herself "princess." That title belonged to Elizabeth.

Mary refused. God had given her the title and the privileges that went with it, she said. Only God could take it away.

Under orders from the king, the advisers cut the size of Mary's household. They took away some of her servants and reduced her income. But the biggest blow was yet to come.

In November, Anne Boleyn's uncle, the Duke of Norfolk, arrived with another message. Mary would be moving to an estate in Hatfield, 20 miles north of London. There, she would become maid of honor to Elizabeth.

"The infant Princess of Wales—" he began, but Mary interrupted him.

"That is a title which belongs to me and no one else," she declared.

But Mary had no choice in the matter. The king had ordered her to move. Mary asked for a year's salary for her servants, who would now be without jobs. Then she boarded a carriage and moved to Hatfield. The Duke of Norfolk saw her to a plain attic room. He asked whether she had a message for the king.

"None, except that the Princess of Wales, his daughter, asked for his blessing," Mary said.

The duke refused to deliver such a message. Mary ordered him to leave and then burst into tears.

Mary was heartbroken. But like her mother, she was determined to face these setbacks with pride. She also had help from her former fiancé, Charles V. Mary and Catherine, of course, were family to Charles. And he considered them his allies in England.

In fact, Charles lent his ambassador in England to Mary and her mother. Eustace Chapuys traveled often between the two women. He advised them both and carried secret messages between them.

Through Chapuys, Catherine told Mary that she must never give up her title. The Catholic Church still considered Catherine and Henry's marriage to be legal. And Mary must remain true to her faith.

Mary had been living in Hatfield for some months when her father visited the castle. Mary was overjoyed. But the king made it clear he would see only Elizabeth. He sent his secretary, Thomas Cromwell, to Mary instead.

Cromwell demanded once again that Mary give up the title of princess. Mary refused. She begged to see her father, but Cromwell would not allow it.

Desperate, Mary climbed to the roof of the castle and waited for her father to come out. When Henry looked up, she was kneeling with her hands clasped before her. He nodded and touched his hat. He was said to have tears in his eyes.

Henry's softness toward his daughter made Anne furious. She ordered that new restrictions be placed on Mary. Mary was to have her face slapped whenever she insisted on being called princess.

Anne even visited Mary to demand her obedience. Mary responded that she knew only one queen of England and that was her mother. Soon after, Anne sent the Duke of Norfolk to take away Mary's jewels and her finest clothes.

When the household left Hatfield a few days later, Mary was still angry. She refused to sit in the carriage behind Elizabeth. She had to be dragged, kicking and screaming, from the castle.

In March 1534, Parliament made Mary's new status official. They passed a law called the Act of Succession. The new law declared Mary to be illegitimate. Henry's children with Anne would be his heirs.

Everyone in the kingdom was ordered to take an oath promising to observe the Act of Succession. Anyone who refused would be arrested and charged with treason. And treason was punishable by death.

Suddenly, Mary and her mother seemed to be in serious danger. Catherine refused to take the oath. If Mary refused as well, would they both be executed?

Mary waited in fear for her father's men to arrive. Before long, nine people had been executed for refusing to take Henry's oath. Would Mary be next? She sent word to Charles, begging him to help her escape England. The emperor refused.

Before Mary could convince him, she suffered another heartbreaking loss.

CHAPTER 6

Heartbroken

MARY LOSES HER MOTHER
and gains a brother.

IN JANUARY 1536, MARY RECEIVED THE news: Her mother had died.

Mary was crushed. She refused to attend the funeral, which she claimed was not fit for a queen.

Henry, on the other hand, reacted with relief at the news of his former wife's death. With Catherine gone, Charles would have no reason to invade England. "Thank God!" Henry cried. "We are now free from any fear of war."

The king had another reason to be hopeful. Anne was pregnant at the time, raising Henry's hopes for a male heir. But his joy was short-lived. Soon after Catherine's death, Anne had a miscarriage.

What's more, Henry's spies told him that Anne had been having affairs. The king was outraged. He had his wife arrested for treason and sent to jail in the Tower of London. Her marriage to Henry was ruled invalid. And her daughter, Elizabeth, was declared illegitimate.

On May 19, 1536, guards led Anne Boleyn from the Tower to be executed. Anne asked that the executioner use a sword rather than a blunt axe to ensure a quick death. "He shall not have much trouble," she told the keepers of the Tower. "I have a little neck."

Just 11 days after Anne's death, Henry married again. His new wife, Jane Seymour, was a kind woman. Mary hoped that the change would open the way to a new start with her father. She wrote to congratulate him on his marriage. She asked his

QUEEN ANNE WAS BEHEADED after Henry accused her of
being unfaithful. Anne's suspected partner was arrested and tortured
until he confessed to the affair.

blessing "in as humble and lowly a manner as is possible." But she stopped short of accepting the Act of Succession.

Henry did not answer. Mary wrote again, begging for a response. Still there was only silence. Cromwell, the king's secretary, told her that Henry still would not see her. He insisted that Mary sign papers agreeing to two points. First, she must say that her father, not the Pope, was head of the Church of England. She must also agree that her parents' marriage had been illegal.

Still, Mary refused to budge.

"I think you are the most [stubborn] woman that ever was," Cromwell wrote her.

Even Charles V now wanted Mary to sign Henry's papers. Chapuys brought her messages from the emperor, urging her to obey her father. She must do it for England, if not for herself, Charles said. If she were executed for treason, it would tear the country apart.

JANE SEYMOUR WAS King Henry's third wife. She gave birth to a male heir, Edward. The baby flourished, but Jane died 12 days later.

Mary did not know what to do. Her mother, she knew, would never have agreed to such terms. But she was scared and alone. She missed her father. Finally, she gave in. She was filled with guilt. But on June 22, she signed her father's papers.

Henry responded immediately. He and Jane visited Mary on July 6. The king and his daughter spent hours talking together. Jane gave Mary a beautiful diamond ring. They shared dinner in Mary's rooms.

When Henry and Jane left, it was with good feelings all around.

By fall, Mary was back at court. She was not yet called princess, but she was once again living like one. She had money and fine clothing and beautiful jewels.

On October 12, 1537, Jane gave birth to Henry's long-desired son. Henry celebrated for days. And Mary accepted it with grace. Always fond of children, she adored little Edward. She was named his godmother at the christening. Elizabeth was there, too, and she and Mary left the service hand in hand.

But Edward's mother fell ill after his birth and never recovered. She died when Edward was 12 days old. Henry had lost a wife, and Mary had lost a good friend. When Jane was buried, Mary took the role of chief mourner.

CHAPTER 7

Back at Court

Mary is back in favor
DURING THE FINAL YEARS OF
HER FATHER'S LIFE.

Finally, KING HENRY HAD HIS HEIR. Mary accepted her fate as the half sister to the future king. She loved Edward and even felt warmly toward Elizabeth. After all, both of them were now illegitimate daughters of the king.

She even accepted Henry's break from the Pope. Henry still considered himself a Catholic. And although Martin Luther was gaining English followers, the Church of England still observed Catholic rituals.

HENRY VIII (left) made his son Edward (center) heir to the throne. Mary and Elizabeth (far right) were declared illegitimate.

Most important to Mary, worshippers were allowed to celebrate Mass—in Latin.

Mary settled into a comfortable life. She spent time with old friends from her childhood. She played cards and spent long hours weaving. She played the virginal and the lute. She hunted, rode her horses, and practiced archery. Her greyhounds were a special pleasure.

Outside the castle walls, religious conflict was heating up. While Henry had no problem with the rituals of Catholicism, he hated the Pope. Henry wanted full control over the Church of England.

HENRY'S SOLDIERS FORCE A GROUP OF TERRIFIED MONKS from their home. Henry began seizing Catholic properties in England. He had some monasteries destroyed and sold others to the wealthy.

Henry began attacking the Pope's English allies. He took over wealthy Catholic monasteries all across England. He sold the land to nobles who then owed their support to the king. Thousands of monks and nuns from the monasteries were forced to work for the Church of England.

Henry's attack on the monasteries enraged a lot of English Catholics. A 67-year-old woman who had been Mary's governess, the Countess of Salisbury, got caught in the middle of the fight. The countess was imprisoned after her son, Reginald Pole, wrote a book criticizing Henry's religious policies. After two years in the Tower of London, the countess was beheaded at the age of 70.

The conflicts outside the castle didn't seem to affect Mary's relationship with her father. Over the next few years, the two of them stayed close. Mary lived at court from time to time. Her father visited her often.

It wasn't long before Henry married again——and again, and again. Between 1540 and 1543, the king took his fourth, fifth, and sixth wives. He divorced the fourth, Anne of Cleves, almost immediately. She had been described to Henry as educated and beautiful. When she arrived for the wedding, Henry decided she was neither and ended the marriage soon after.

Henry's fifth wife, Catherine Howard, fared even worse. She lasted for a year and a half before Henry accused her of having an affair. She was beheaded in the Tower.

The sixth wife, Catherine Parr, was a better match. She was a Protestant, but Mary was fond of her. Catherine loved children and took an interest in Edward and Elizabeth. She educated them both in her religion.

By December 1546, Henry's health was failing. He made a new will. Edward would take over the throne upon his death. Mary would be next in line, and Elizabeth third.

Henry also named a council to help Edward rule until he was old enough to do so himself. Mary was not worried about her brother's Protestant beliefs. She was sure that he would come back to the Catholic faith. His council included Protestant advisers. But that did not worry her either. Their job was not to change things. It was simply to keep watch until Edward was old enough to make decisions on his own.

Mary herself had no desire to rule. Her brother was quiet and serious. She was convinced the country would be in good hands when he took over.

A New King

EDWARD TAKES THE THRONE,
and Mary does not like what she sees.

WHEN HER FATHER DIED IN JANUARY
1547, Mary was almost 31. For the first time in her
life, she was free to live her own life. She inherited
vast estates from her father. Most of her land lay 80
miles northeast of London in the county of Norfolk.
Mary traveled often between her properties. Wherever
she went, people greeted her with warmth.

But in the summer, she heard distressing news
from London. Edward's councilors were beginning
to wipe out hundreds of years of Catholic tradition.

They ordered crosses removed from churches. Psalms were being sung in English instead of Latin. Some of the council members did not even go to Mass.

Mary was horrified. She had assumed that the Church of England would be almost identical to the Catholic Church—only without the Pope. Quickly, Mary wrote a letter of protest to the council. Her father had left the realm in "Godly order and Quietness," she said. The council had no right to disrupt it by ordering changes in church practice.

Mary's letter made the council members furious. They began to worry that Mary might stir up anger among Catholics. They insisted that they were only continuing the work Henry had begun. They also told Mary that she could worship as she liked, as long as she did so privately.

Mary did exactly that—until Protestant leaders took the next step. Parliament, which rarely disagreed with the king's council, passed the Act of Uniformity in January 1549. The new law made it illegal for priests to celebrate the Catholic Mass. Instead, during the worship service, believers were to read from Archbishop Cranmer's new Book of Common Prayer—which was written in English.

Mary was furious. She rode about her estates telling priests to ignore the new law. On the day the

IN THE CHURCH OF ENGLAND, WORSHIPPERS READ from the Book of Common Prayer. This book, as well as the actual worship service, were in English. The Catholic Mass was in Latin.

law became official, Mary held a Catholic Mass in her chapel. Anyone who wished to attend was invited.

Before long, a huge protest had begun. In the west of England, people insisted their priests say Mass in Latin. The so-called Prayer Book Rebellion swept across the counties of Devon and Cornwall. Armed rebels sent their demands to the council. They wanted the Catholic rituals restored and crosses returned to their churches.

Mary was scolded by the council for holding her public Mass. But the Holy Roman Emperor defended Mary. Charles told his ambassador to send a message to the council. His cousin must not be forced to "change her religion," he insisted.

The council took Charles's message as a threat. Would he invade England and try to place Mary on the throne? A force of 8,000 English soldiers gathered to guard the coast. Mary feared for her life again. She begged Charles once more to help her escape. And finally, her cousin agreed to help.

Mary traveled to Essex on the coast. There, she waited for a Spanish ship to take her away. In July 1550, Charles sent a representative named Jehan Dubois, disguised as a corn merchant. But when Dubois arrived on the coast and sent word to Mary, she panicked. How could she leave all her friends? And what about the English Catholics who needed her leadership? She couldn't decide what to do.

When Dubois arrived at Mary's home, she was sick with worry. She could not go now, she told him. Perhaps the next day or the day after that. But as they talked, a message arrived. Their plan had been discovered. Dubois was forced to hurry away. He left Mary wringing her hands and crying, "What shall we do? What is to become of me?"

CHAPTER 9

Bloodless Revolution

Will Mary become queen AT LAST?

KING EDWARD'S COUNCIL HAD INDEED learned about Charles's plan to rescue Mary. And they decided to tighten their control over her.

The council was now headed by the Duke of Northumberland, who had strong Protestant leanings. He had brought several Protestants onto the council with him. Mary considered Northumberland and his supporters to be dangerous. She said they "fear no God and respect no persons."

Northumberland insisted that Mary come to London, where the council could keep watch over her. Mary said no. But when a letter arrived from the king himself, Mary could not refuse.

Still, she managed to turn her visit into a protest. She entered London with a crowd of supporters. They carried rosaries and other symbols of their Catholic faith.

At the castle, Mary got a cold greeting from her half brother. Edward was just 13, but he had begun to act like a king. Angrily, he told his adult sister that she must stop disobeying the law.

Mary insisted that she had to be true to her faith.

Edward replied harshly. He did not care about her faith. But he did care about her actions, he said. By defying him, Mary made him look weak. It was time for her to stop.

Mary left without giving in. She had insulted the king to his face. And Northumberland began to take revenge. He arrested members of Mary's household and held them in jail. He sent council members to insist that Mary obey the law.

But Mary was convinced that she had God on her side. Her faith was the most important thing in her life. She spent long hours in prayer. She often celebrated Mass four times a day. She vowed that she'd help England return to the Roman Catholic Church.

MARY WAS WILLING TO RISK HER LIFE to defend her faith. At her estates in Norfolk, she prayed for hours each day. Meanwhile, her brother King Edward began to arrest her supporters.

Little did she know how soon her chance would come.

In 1553, Mary received word that Edward was dying. He had been ill off and on for months. Now it was clear: There would be no heir for Edward VI, male or female. According to Henry's will, Mary was next in line to rule England.

But before long Mary heard rumors that Edward and Northumberland were plotting against her. Edward wanted to change his father's will. Mary and Elizabeth would be taken out of line. Instead, Henry's grandniece, Lady Jane Grey, would take the throne. Lady Jane was a Protestant. And she had just been married, with great speed, to Northumberland's son, Guildford Dudley. So, after Edward's death, Jane would become queen.

On July 1, 1553, false rumors reached Mary that Edward was dead. She felt sure Northumberland would try to arrest her. In the dark of night she set out. She and a small party rode hard toward Norfolk.

THE DUKE OF NORTHUMBERLAND CONVINCES Jane Grey to take the crown. Soon Mary would also declare herself queen. Which woman would win the battle for the English throne?

There, in the center of her estates, she would be surrounded by supporters.

On July 6, Edward finally died. Events began to move quickly. Four days later, in London, Northumberland and his council assembled in public. They declared Jane Grey queen. The crowd gave them a cool response.

The next night, in Norfolk, Mary gathered her household around her. She proclaimed herself Queen of England. According to one account, "Everyone, both the gently born and the humbler servants, cheered her to the rafters."

From London, Northumberland set off with 1,500 soldiers to arrest Mary. But armed men had already begun arriving at Mary's home to declare their support for her. Mary moved her army to Suffolk, where she found more men waiting for her. In a matter of days, Mary had raised an army of 30,000.

Northumberland's supporters began to realize that they were backing the wrong person. The people of England wanted Mary as their queen. On July 18, a group of council members met in London. They declared Northumberland a traitor.

On July 19, Mary was proclaimed queen. Not a shot had been fired. There was rejoicing in the streets of London. Mary was finally in a position to bring England back to the Catholic Church.

Mary Tudor in Pictures

MARY'S FATHER
Henry VIII, King of England, King of Ireland, Prince of Wales, musician, poet, gambler, and Defender of the Faith. Henry also claimed to be the King of France.

COSTLY DIVORCE
Catherine of Aragon, Mary's mother. When Catherine didn't produce a male heir, Henry tried to divorce her. But the Pope refused to give his permission, and so Henry broke from the Catholic Church.

ROYAL EDUCATION
When Mary was nine, her father sent her to Ludlow Castle near Wales, to be trained as a princess.

END OF QUEEN ANNE
Henry accused his second wife, Anne, of adultery, treason, and witchcraft, and had her beheaded in 1536.

HENRY GETS HIS HEIR
Henry became engaged to Jane Seymour the day after Anne was beheaded. In 1537, Jane gave birth to Edward.

PIOUS PRINCESS
Mary had a lonely childhood, but her strong Catholic faith gave her comfort.

PROTESTANT PUPPET

After Henry's death in 1547, Mary's nine-year-old brother became King Edward VI. The boy's advisers pushed English worshippers further from the Catholic Church.

CATHOLIC EMPEROR

Charles V was Mary's cousin and ally. He ruled over nearly half of Europe.

INFORMATION AGE

The invention of the printing press helped fuel the Protestant Reformation. Now that the Bible was widely available, people could interpret it their own way—not just rely on the Catholic Church to tell them its message.

ONCE OUTCAST, NOW QUEEN

In 1553, Queen Mary (center) enters London in triumph, with Elizabeth following behind her.

NINE-DAY REIGN

After Edward's death, Jane Grey had declared herself queen. After Mary became queen, she ordered Jane beheaded.

UNWANTED PRINCE

Mary took Charles's advice and married his son Philip in 1554. But the marriage angered Parliament, which didn't want a Spanish ruler.

GOD'S PUNISHMENT?

As queen, Mary suffered from mysterious health problems. She worried that God was punishing her.

A PRISON FOR THE PROTESTANTS

Mary had many people imprisoned in the Tower of London, including her sister, Elizabeth.

ON THE RACK

Convinced that she was carrying out the will of God, Mary had some Protestants tortured.

TRIAL BY FIRE

Bloody Mary had hundreds of Protestants burned at the stake. The killings threatened to tear England apart.

QUEEN ELIZABETH

Elizabeth became queen after Mary's death in 1558. She reversed Mary's religious reforms, and her reign became known as the Golden Age.

PART 3

Bloody Mary

C H A P T E R   1 0

Queen at Last

MARY WINS THE CROWN
and begins her reign.

MARY WAS QUEEN AT LAST. SHE BEGAN
the trip from Suffolk to London. Several hundred guards
rode with her. A parade of supporters followed behind.

Her journey was interrupted by a stream of
visitors. Common people came to offer gifts to the
queen. Council members arrived from London to beg
forgiveness. Jane Grey's mother asked Mary to treat
her daughter with mercy.

The ambassadors of Charles V, led by Simon
Renard, had words of caution for Mary. Renard warned

the queen to move slowly with her religious reforms. Many people in England worshipped as Protestants now, he said. If Mary attacked their faith, she might spark a revolt.

AFTER PARLIAMENT DECLARED HER the rightful queen, Mary (center) entered London in triumph. Her reunion with her sister, Elizabeth (right), was a happy one.

Mary did not take Renard's advice well. She would not do anything without the approval of Parliament, she said. However, she owed her new position to God. She must show her gratitude by bringing the true faith back to England.

Mary's last visitor was perhaps the most important. As Mary approached London, Elizabeth rode out to meet her and knelt before the queen with her head bowed. Mary had not seen her half sister in several years. She told Elizabeth to stand and embraced her warmly. When Mary set off again, Elizabeth rode in the place of honor directly behind her.

In London, Mary faced the business of ruling a country. She had never participated in council meetings. She had never looked at state papers. Suddenly she had crucial decisions to make.

Mary dealt with Northumberland first. She put the duke and two of his supporters on trial for treason. They were convicted and executed in August 1553. She placed Lady Jane Grey and her husband, Guildford, in the Tower. But no one else was punished for their involvement in the plot.

Renard told Mary she should have been harsher. How did she expect to keep order if people did not fear her? As England's first female ruler, she already faced great challenges. Being soft on traitors would make her look weak. But Mary would not change her mind.

Mary did take Charles's advice on the religious issue. She freed Catholics who were in jail for protesting Edward's reforms. But she moved slowly to bring back all the Catholic rituals. Parliament would not meet until October. She would wait for them to approve changes in church policy.

Elizabeth was another problem. More and more she reminded Mary of Anne Boleyn. And worse, Elizabeth would not attend Mass. Finally, Mary threatened to confine her half sister to the Tower.

Elizabeth came weeping to the queen. She had been brought up Protestant, Elizabeth cried. She did not know any other way. She begged Mary to help her learn about the Catholic Mass.

Mary softened. But Elizabeth's interest didn't last long. Mary began to wonder: Was Elizabeth plotting with the Protestants to overthrow her?

On October 1, Mary was formally crowned in London. She wore a blue velvet gown and a gold cap with jewels and pearls. Six horses pulled her chariot, which was covered in cloth of gold. Flowers were thrown on the streets, and tapestries hung from windows along the route. Leading Mary was a long line of knights, gentlemen, clergy, and council members. Behind her rode Elizabeth and other relatives. Forty-six ladies-in-waiting rode beside them dressed in crimson satin.

At Westminster Abbey, a bishop put a crown made specially for Mary on her head. It weighed seven pounds.

After the coronation, Queen Mary held her first public Mass in London. It was, after all, her country now. And she would worship as she pleased.

Mary's Mission

The queen tries to bring the Mass—
and a husband—TO ENGLAND.

MARY WAS CONVINCED THAT GOD HAD
put her on the throne for a reason—to bring
England back to the Catholic Church. At last, she
could attend to her goal. First she had to get rid of
Edward's religious reforms. Then she had to produce
a Catholic heir.

Parliament met in October 1553. At Mary's insistence,
its members declared the marriage of her parents,
Henry and Catherine, to be legal. Finally, Mary was
once again a royal daughter under English law.

Next, Parliament discussed the possible return of the Catholic rituals. Would English priests be allowed to celebrate Mass? Would the Book of Common Prayer be banned? Would services once again be held in Latin? The debate was long and heated.

Mary quickly took aim at her adversaries. She had several important leaders imprisoned for protesting her religious policies. Archbishop Thomas Cranmer, for instance, had helped Henry divorce Mary's mother. Now he was jailed in the Tower of London.

While Parliament debated, Mary had a more personal problem to resolve. Thirty-five years after her first engagement, she was determined to marry.

As queen, Mary could choose her own husband. But the idea of marriage made her uneasy. At 37, she was not a young woman. Age and illness had made their mark on her. She was nearly toothless, and she was thin from constant stomach problems.

Besides, a queen did not marry just for herself. She married for her country. And England had a lot at stake. The country had never had a ruling queen. No one knew just how much power Mary's husband would have. Would he become ruler of the kingdom? Would he take over if the queen died without an heir? This became an even bigger question if Mary married a ruler from another country. Would England become part of her husband's kingdom?

The decision was complicated, and Mary dealt with it in a familiar way. She turned to Charles for advice.

Charles acted the way any good emperor would. He picked his own son, Philip. The emperor, now a widower, would have married Mary himself, Renard told the queen. But he thought he was too old and unwell.

Philip seemed like an even stranger choice to Mary. He was 11 years younger than Mary. And she had heard he was not as wise as his father. He was a good Catholic. But he was Spanish. She did not think her council would approve of that. She told Renard to thank the emperor. The match was a good one. But she would have to think about it.

Renard assured her that the prince would make a great husband. He was very mature for his years. He was "as virtuous as any prince in this world."

Renard returned later with a written proposal from Charles. Mary was so nervous she could hardly speak. She had been weeping and praying for hours, she told Renard in a whisper. She took the papers and disappeared again.

When Mary met with Renard in the morning, she had her answer. She said she had prayed all night. She had been inspired by God. She would marry Prince Philip.

Mary was overcome by the stress of her decision. She agreed to wait to announce the engagement. Then she fell ill for the next ten days. The official word was that the weather was to blame. But some people whispered that the queen was sick this way every year. It was "from the womb," people said. They began to worry whether the queen would ever have an heir.

In November, Mary got what she wanted from Parliament. They passed laws bringing Catholic rituals back to the English Church. But they were fearful that Mary might marry a man from another country. Several members of Parliament urged her to take a British husband. Mary grew angry. She appeared before Parliament and reminded its members that they had no say in the matter when kings married. Why should it be any different with a queen? She could marry whomever she chose, she insisted.

Finally on January 18, 1554, Mary's engagement to Philip was announced. The reaction was swift and very angry.

CHAPTER 12

A Spanish Prince

The people rebel at Mary's choice and
PLOT TO OVERTHROW HER.

JUST THREE DAYS AFTER HER ENGAGEMENT
was announced, Mary learned of a plot against her.
A group of men had been planning for months to
overthrow her and put Elizabeth on the throne.
Now, with the people furious over Mary's Spanish
fiancé, the plotters were ready to act. The rebellion
was planned for March 18, 1554.

A knight named Thomas Wyatt had agreed to
lead the uprising in Kent. Wyatt had spent time in
Spain. He had seen the fearsome Spanish Inquisition

firsthand. The Inquisition was a kind of religious court. Its judges dealt harshly with people who did not follow the rules of the Catholic Church. Thousands of people had been burned at the stake for heresy. Mary's engagement had made some people wonder: Was their queen planning to bring the Inquisition to England?

Wyatt gathered 3,000 men and started marching toward London. Mary quickly sent troops to put down

THOMAS WYATT'S ARMY INVADES London. Wyatt believed Mary and Philip would bring the bloody Inquisition to England.

the rebellion. Her soldiers met Wyatt at Rochester Bridge, just 25 miles outside of London, on January 29. But Wyatt convinced the queen's troops to join him.

The situation did not look good for Mary. With Wyatt approaching fast, she had to stop the people of London from joining the rebellion. On February 1, Mary put on her crown and robes and addressed a public gathering. Hundreds of people crowded into a hall. She looked out and spoke to them calmly and firmly. She loved her people "as a mother doth love her child," she declared. She expected that the people loved her the same way. Together, she ended hopefully, "we shall give these rebels a short and speedy overthrow."

The crowd roared their approval. They set to work at once preparing the city against attack. When Wyatt reached London Bridge on February 3, he found it closed. He waited another three days, hoping for support from within London. When none came, he marched up the river to Kingston Bridge. By then the people had organized an army to fight him. He had no choice but to surrender. Wyatt and 500 of his men were arrested for treason.

Mary thanked God for yet another miracle. But she had learned a hard lesson. Some of the plotters were friends of Jane Grey and Guildford Dudley. They were men she had freed when she became queen. This time Mary would not be so foolish. She would put down these rebels once and for all and make it safe for Philip to come to England.

Mary had Wyatt beheaded and 150 of his men hanged. Jane Grey and her husband Guildford Dudley were also executed. Mary ordered Elizabeth to the Tower while her role in the rebellion was investigated.

Mary had put down the first challenge to her reign. Now, she waited to hear from Philip. God willing, he would arrive safely. Hopefully he would give her an heir that would keep the throne out of her sister's hands for good.

CHAPTER 13

The Royal Couple

Mary meets her new fiancé—
AND THIS ONE SHE MARRIES.

WHILE MARY WAITED FOR PHILIP, THE members of Parliament worked out the details of her reign. They decided that she would have the same powers as a king. Her property would pass directly to her heir rather than to her husband. That would keep the kingdom out of Spanish hands.

But Mary was still having trouble getting everything she wanted from Parliament. It refused to bring back the old heresy laws that would make it legal to burn Protestants at the stake. And Mary was tiring of the fights between Protestant and Catholic members of her council. She spent all her time shouting at her council, she told Renard. She was sure Philip would be able to solve these problems for her—if only he would come to England soon.

As Philip's arrival neared, Mary began to feel more cheerful. It appeared that Elizabeth had known nothing about the Wyatt Rebellion. Mary began feeling warmer toward her sister. She rehung Elizabeth's portrait in the palace. In May 1554, she released Elizabeth from the Tower.

Finally, on July 23, the day Mary had long awaited came. Philip arrived at Winchester, where the wedding was to be held. Mary waited anxiously. She had never met her husband. She had only a portrait of him that Renard had found for her.

It was 10 P.M. before she finally heard his footsteps. Mary descended a set of stairs and met him before members of her court. He was slim and blond with a trim yellow beard. He smiled and kissed Mary. Then the couple sat and began to talk. He did not speak English. She understood Spanish but did not speak it well. They both knew Latin, and they managed to stay up chatting well into the night.

On July 25, they were married in the Winchester Cathedral. The royal couple left the church hand in hand.

Mary wrote to the emperor to thank him. Philip, she said, was "so full of virtues that the realm's honor and [peace] will certainly be . . . increased."

Mary and Philip spent the first week at Winchester. Mary rose at dawn each day for Mass. She worked at the business of the country until after midnight. She suffered from headaches and her usual stomach problems. But still, she was happy. Philip was able to help her with the affairs of state. And he was kind to her. Mary, who had not had much love in her life, enjoyed his attention.

Mary knew that the English people were still suspicious of her husband. But the people were

QUEEN MARY AND HER HUSBAND, PHILIP OF SPAIN. Although Mary was in poor health, she was happier than she had ever been.

hopeful that the couple would produce an heir. When Mary and Philip returned to London, they were met by cheering crowds.

Then, in September, the miracle that Mary had prayed for seemed to be granted. The royal doctor declared that she was pregnant. All the signs were there. She was nauseated, and her belly seemed to be swelling. Mary was overjoyed. In October, Philip wrote to his father telling him the news. There would be an heir.

A Lot at Stake

England becomes Catholic again, and
MARY GOES AFTER HER ENEMIES.

Near the end of 1554, everything was going as Mary had prayed. Philip convinced the Pope to drop his claims to the monastery lands that Henry had taken. In exchange, Parliament agreed to let England be welcomed back into the Catholic Church.

Mary and Philip went to Westminster Palace to open Parliament. One of Philip's men observed that marriage was treating Mary well. "The queen is fatter and has better color than when she wasn't married," he wrote. "Indeed she is said to be very happy."

At Parliament, Mary received an envoy from the Pope. The man was Cardinal Reginald Pole, the son of Mary's former governess. Long ago, Pole had criticized King Henry's religious policies. Henry had executed Pole's mother for her son's crimes. Pole himself had been living in exile for 15 years. Now, thanks to Mary, he had returned.

Pole knelt before the queen and spoke the words from the Hail Mary. "Blessed among women, and blessed be the fruit of your womb," he said. Mary gasped, thinking she felt the child in her womb leap in response.

When Parliament opened, the members formally asked the Catholic Church for forgiveness. Cardinal Pole then welcomed England back into the church.

Parliament, however, was not yet finished. It passed the last of Mary's religious laws. It would now be illegal for Protestants to preach. Priests would once again not be allowed to marry. The Book of Common Prayer would be banned. People who printed Protestant

A CROWD WATCHES AS JOHN ROGERS IS BURNED ALIVE.
Rogers was the first to die for refusing to obey Mary's laws
against Protestantism.

writings would lose their presses. And finally, anyone breaking these laws could be burned at the stake.

Christmas that year was the happiest of Mary's life. She finally had the power to stop heresy in England. And she would soon have an heir.

The people of England, however, did not accept Mary's new laws peacefully. Many Protestants immediately fled England for France or the Holy Roman Empire. Many who stayed rose up in protest. In London a man who spoke out in favor of the Mass was stabbed. In Suffolk a church was burned while the people inside heard Mass.

Mary acted quickly to stop the protests. Guards arrested anyone who questioned the new laws. In January, Mary's bishops put the prisoners on trial.

John Rogers, the priest who had married and was practicing Protestantism, was the first to be found guilty. Four more Protestant leaders followed. All were offered a chance to accept Catholicism. They refused.

Rogers died quickly at the stake while his family

watched. John Hooper, the Bishop of Worcester and Gloucester, was not so fortunate. He went to the stake on February 9, 1555. A crowd of 7,000 came to watch him die. Hooper forgave the executioner for what he was about to do and prepared to die. But it was a windy day. The wood placed around the stake was green and burned poorly. The wind blew the flames away from Hooper's body. At first, only his legs were burned.

More wood was sent for, but still it burned slowly. "For God's love, good people," Hooper pleaded, "let me have more fire." He burned for three-quarters of an hour before he finally died.

The Catholics in the crowd said that it was God's will that Hooper should suffer so. Mary agreed. She believed that everyone would see the burnings as a warning from God and turn away from heresy.

But for Protestants, John Hooper's death had the opposite effect. Many of them left the scene inspired by the strength of the bishop's faith. For Mary, the struggle would be harder than she had hoped.

CHAPTER 15

Burned Alive

As more heretics go to the stake, Mary has a baby. OR DOES SHE?

IN MARCH 1555, A DOZEN MORE HERETICS were burned.

The following month, Mary and Philip moved their household to Hampton Court. At the end of the month, Mary retired from public view to wait for her baby to be born. A pregnant woman was not to be seen in public. While she seemed to be in good health, she was now 39. In those days, most women had stopped giving birth by then. It was likely that she'd have a difficult delivery—or even die in childbirth.

PROTESTANTS ARE LED TO LONDON for their trials. People wondered whether Mary meant to kill every Protestant in England.

Finally, on April 30, news spread that Mary had given birth to a healthy son. The queen, it was said, was out of danger. In the streets of London, bonfires were lit. Bells rang out across the city. When the news reached the emperor, his court celebrated.

The news, however, was untrue. Doctors said they had been wrong about the child's due date. But Mary's midwife hinted that the royal doctor was avoiding the truth. There was no child.

April passed into May and then to June. Still there was no child.

In those three months, ten more heretics died. Most people in England approved of the burnings.

But there were also rumors of Protestant plots against Mary. Spectators at some of the burnings cried out that the heretics were holy martyrs. They copied down the victims' last words. When the fires burned out, these Protestants searched through the ashes looking for remains of the bodies to keep as holy treasures.

Still at home, waiting to give birth, Mary wept over her prayer book. She left tearstains on the page with the prayer for the safe delivery of a child. On June 1, she felt labor pains, but they soon passed. Her doctors assured her she would have her baby in July.

June passed into July. Another ten Protestants were burned. Rumors about the queen passed around London. People said she believed that every heretic in prison had to be burned before her child could be born. Protests broke out over the burnings. Troops had to be called in to put them down.

In August, the mood in England grew worse. Heavy rains ruined the harvest. Grain rotted in the fields. Cows and horses starved for lack of hay and oats. Soon the people, too, would be hungry.

That month, 18 more prisoners died. Now it was not just important clergymen going to the stake. The victims were mostly common people. Mary had been convinced that the Protestants had bewitched her, people said. She had told her bishops to kill them all.

For Mary, nothing was going right. At last, she had to admit that she was not pregnant. It's not clear what caused her symptoms. But it was not a baby.

Mary was convinced, as always, that God was trying to tell her something. The poor harvest and her failure to produce a baby were signs that He was not happy with her. She would have to work harder to rid the kingdom of heretics.

PHANTOM CHILD

PRODUCING A MALE HEIR WAS A QUEEN'S most important job. Daughters usually did not grow up to rule countries. If a son was not born, the queen was always to blame.

But childbirth was a dangerous business in the 1500s—for the mother and for the child. One in ten women died in childbirth. And most women had seven or more pregnancies.

Doctors at the time knew very little. Women who could not get pregnant were sometimes told to drink the urine of pregnant sheep or goats. Some wore the bones of stillborn children under their clothes as charms to help them get pregnant.

Even so, what could explain Mary's false pregnancy? In those days, there were no good pregnancy tests. Mary probably had some kind of illness in her reproductive organs. Chances are, doctors didn't check her carefully. Usually, they were not allowed to physically examine a queen.

MARY HAD UNEXPLAINED health problems her entire life.

CHAPTER 16

Alone Again

PHILIP DEPARTS, LEAVING MARY to battle plotters and heretics.

AT THE END OF AUGUST 1555, MARY suffered another blow. Philip decided to leave England. He had problems to deal with in the Netherlands. And he felt like an outsider in Mary's country. It angered him that Parliament had not given him full powers as king.

Mary said goodbye to Philip as he boarded a boat. He promised to return soon. Mary held herself together long enough to return to her room. There, people saw her weeping at the window until Philip's ship was out of sight.

Mary wrote to Philip almost daily. And she kept signing execution papers. Fourteen convicted heretics died in September. On October 16, two men who had been in prison since the beginning of Mary's reign were sent to the stake. One was Nicholas Ridley, the former Bishop of London. The other was Hugh Latimer, the former Bishop of Worcester.

"Be of good comfort, Master Ridley," Latimer said as they were chained to the stake. "We shall this day light such a candle . . . as I trust shall never be put out." Latimer died quickly that day, but Ridley suffered a slow death in a badly built fire.

Mary continued to hope that the deaths would turn Protestants back to the Catholic Church. But the real truth lay in Latimer's words. Each burning made a new martyr. And each new martyr made English Protestants more determined to resist Mary's terror.

Early in 1556, Mary got word of a new plot against her. Henry Dudley, a distant relative of Lady Jane Grey, was one of the leaders. His plan was to get help from

France. The French king, Henry II, would provide money. Dudley would organize a force from among the hundreds of English Protestants who had fled to France. They would invade England from the south while others began a rebellion within the country. After they defeated Mary, they would make Elizabeth queen.

The plot began to fail when Henry II refused to fund it. Charles had just made Philip king of Spain. And Philip had made peace with France. King Henry did not want to anger his new ally.

In March the plot fell apart when Mary's councilors discovered the plan. About 20 of the plotters were sent to the Tower. Mary was shaken and the council was alarmed. The men involved were too close to Mary's inner circle for comfort. She no longer knew who to trust. Fearing for her life, she began keeping armed guards in her private rooms.

Mary wrote to Charles begging that Philip return to England. Charles promised to send his son back soon. But Philip refused to return until he was given all the powers of a king. And Parliament was not ready to put the country in the hands of a Spaniard.

Mary spent her days weeping. She could no longer sleep more than a few hours a night. The French ambassador noted that she had seemed to age ten years since her husband left.

Over the spring and early summer, 66 more Protestants were killed. One victim was a pregnant woman. Another was the former archbishop of

AS MARY AGED, her health deteriorated, and she had trouble sleeping.

Canterbury, Thomas Cranmer. The archbishop was an old man by now. He was loved by many all across England. Protestants hailed him as a martyr to their cause.

Mary continued to write to the emperor, pleading for Philip's return. The country was in a "miserable" state without its king, she said. Still, Philip refused to come back. In a fit of anger, Mary reportedly slashed a portrait of her husband.

Five people were executed in August and five in September. Ten more prisoners died in October, six at the stake and four in prison.

That fall, Philip's truce with France collapsed. Now Philip needed Mary. He wanted her to send troops to France to help him fight a war. Parliament wasn't happy about the request. But Mary was eager to show that she was a loyal wife. She couldn't make Philip a true king of England. But she could send him soldiers.

CHAPTER 17

War!

Mary suffers two more losses— ABROAD AND AT HOME.

IT WAS MARCH 1557 BEFORE PHILIP FINALLY returned to England. Mary was delighted, though she knew he would not stay long. She and Philip began meeting with her councilors to get support for Spain in its war with France.

The burnings seemed to slow for a while. There were seven in January, none in February or March, and only five through April and May. Then, in June, 25 men and women were burned alive.

On July 3, Mary said goodbye to her husband at Dover. Philip's business in England was done. Parliament had offered to send troops to France. Philip boarded a sailing ship and crossed the English Channel to Brussels. More than 7,000 English soldiers joined him there and were soon at war.

From England, Mary followed news of the war closely. Centuries before, England had controlled much of France. By Mary's reign, its territory there had dwindled to a single city, called Calais. In December, Calais fell under attack, and Mary's worst fear came true. The city was forced to surrender to French troops.

Mary had lost England's last territory on the European mainland. She was heartbroken.

Yet at the same time, Mary found something to make her happy. She wrote to Philip to announce that she was pregnant again. She had waited months to tell him, she said, because she wanted to make sure this time.

Philip replied joyfully to the news. "It has gone far to lighten the sorrow I have felt for the loss of Calais," he said.

In England, Catholics claimed that Calais was betrayed to the French by its Protestant governor. During the second half of the year, Mary approved another 45 executions.

IN JANUARY 1558, FRENCH TROOPS CAPTURED Calais,
the last English territory on the mainland of Europe.
Mary blamed Protestants for the defeat.

Mary kept out of the public eye to await the birth of her baby. She was now 42 years old. And once again, she was disappointed. By May 1558, it was clear that she was not pregnant. She may have had a tumor or some other illness. She may have wanted a child so badly that her body showed signs of pregnancy.

In any case, when the truth became clear, Mary sank into depression. She had failed her husband, her country, and God. She begged Philip not to be angry with her. "That will be worse than death for me," she said, "for I have already begun to taste your anger all too often, to my great sorrow."

Philip sent word that he would not be coming back to England soon. Still, Mary ordered ships to wait for him at Dunkirk and Dover. She insisted that rooms between the coast and London be kept ready for his return.

The Queen Is Dead

MARY DIES ALONE, and the fires
finally go out across England.

IN THE SUMMER OF 1558, MARY GREW
sick with fever and seizures. She recovered for
short periods. But she grew weaker as the months
wore on. On October 28, she changed her will.
She had realized that God was not going to give
her a child. And she agreed that the crown would
go to Elizabeth.

Mary made a few last requests in her will. She
asked that her half sister be kind to the queen's
servants and pay the Crown's debts. She also pleaded

that Elizabeth not turn the country away from the Catholic Church.

Philip knew his wife was dying. But he was too busy to return to her side. The war with France was finally ending. Philip had to negotiate the peace. Besides, Charles had died in September. Philip needed to take care of the funeral.

While she was able, Mary continued to approve executions. Nine Protestants were burned in July, three in August, and the final 11 in November.

Mary left no sign of regret over the deaths. Her one great sorrow was the loss of Calais. "When I am dead and opened," she said, "you shall find Calais lying in my heart."

In November, Mary lay near death. She told her ladies that she saw little children like angels playing before her and singing. On November 17, she woke for Mass. She spoke more clearly than she had in days. She watched the priest perform the ceremony. And then she closed her eyes and died.

Elizabeth was named queen that same day. The people of London celebrated in the streets with feasting and bonfires.

It soon became clear that Elizabeth was not going to honor Mary's last requests. She stopped the burnings immediately and released all Protestants who were still in prison.

AFTER QUEEN MARY'S DEATH, the new queen, Elizabeth, turned back all of Mary's religious reforms.

Elizabeth did not want to start a religious war. So she moved slowly in her reforms. Still, she made her goals known from the start. Early in her reign, she attended a Christmas celebration in Whitehall. A priest raised the communion wafer and declared it transformed into the body of Jesus. Elizabeth rose angrily from her seat and stormed out of the hall. It was clear to all that Mary's dream of a Roman Catholic England had finally come to an end.

~~~~~~~~~~~~~~~~~
Wicked?
~~~~~~~~~~~~~~~~~

After Mary's death, Elizabeth made sure that her sister's crimes were not forgotten. A Protestant named John Foxe wrote a book called the *Book of Martyrs*. It described the deaths of the people Mary had executed for heresy. Elizabeth insisted that every church in England keep a copy of the book. The book's story helped earn the first ruling queen of England the nickname "Bloody Mary."

During her five years as queen of England, Mary had 300 people executed. In her time it was not an uncommon practice. Both her father and brother had people killed for their beliefs. But more people were executed for heresy under Mary's reign than at any other time in English history.

Yet Mary was said to be a kind and generous woman. She had a deep faith in God. That faith, and the rituals of the Roman Catholic Church, were her

MARY TUDOR:
What she saw as
a divine mission
left no room for
tolerance.

only comfort through a difficult childhood. She loved children and desperately wanted one of her own. She was kind to her servants and gave money to the poor. While queen, she attended the sick and prayed for their healing.

Like her mother before her, she was full of contradictions. Maybe that's why the rhyme, "Mary, Mary, quite contrary," came to be associated with her.

She could be kind, and yet she was brutal to those who did not share her faith. She was a woman of strong beliefs, and yet she did not trust herself to run the country without her husband by her side.

Mary's reign could be called a failure. She had one goal when she became queen: Stop the spread of Protestantism in England. She failed to do it. But as England's first ruling queen, she broke ground for women rulers for centuries to come. In fact, her half sister, Elizabeth, would go on to become one of the most beloved and respected monarchs in British history.

In the end, Mary truly believed that God approved of the executions. She thought the deaths would help turn England away from the Protestant faith. And that would save thousands of people from a fate worse than death. Instead, she gave the Protestants hundreds of new martyrs—and left 300 families to mourn the loss of someone they loved.

Timeline of Terror

1516

1517: Martin Luther nails his Ninety-five Theses to a church door, sparking the Protestant Reformation.

1522: Mary is engaged to Charles V, head of the Holy Roman Empire.

1533: Henry divorces Mary's mother Catherine and marries Anne Boleyn. Anne's daughter, Elizabeth, replaces Mary as princess and heir.

1536: Anne Boleyn is beheaded, and Mary is restored as heir.

October 12, 1537: Henry's new wife, Jane Seymour, gives birth to a son, Edward.

January 1547: Henry VIII dies; Edward VI, Mary's half brother, becomes king.

January 1549: Parliament makes it illegal for priests to celebrate Catholic Mass; Mary protests.

July 1553: King Edward dies; Mary becomes queen.

February 1554: Thomas Wyatt's rebellion against Mary is put down.

July 1554: Mary and Prince Philip of Spain are married.

November 1554: England rejoins the Catholic Church.

February 1555: The first Protestant is burned for heresy.

Summer 1555: After months of anticipation, Mary admits she is not pregnant.

March 1556: Dudley conspiracy fails to overthrow Mary.

July 1557: Mary sends troops to support Philip in war against France.

November 1558: Last of heresy victims is burned at the stake.

January 1558: Calais is forced to surrender to the French.

1558

GLOSSARY

adversary (AD-ver-sehr-ee) *noun* someone who fights or argues against another

ambassador (am-BASS-uh-dur) *noun* a person sent by a government to represent that government in another country

archbishop (arch-BISH-uhp) *noun* in some Christian religions, a senior priest with higher status than a bishop

alliance (uh-LYE-uhnss) *noun* a friendly agreement to work together

communion (kuh-MYOO-nyuhn) *noun* a Christian service in which people eat bread and drink wine or grape juice to remember the last meal of Jesus

emperor (EM-pur-ur) *noun* the male ruler of an empire

envoy (ON-voy) *noun* a person appointed to represent one government in its dealings with another

estate (ess-TATE) *noun* a large area of land, usually with a house on it

execute (ek-suh-KYOOT) *verb* to kill someone as punishment for a crime

heir (AIR) *noun* the person next in line to the throne

heresy (HER-uh-see) *noun* a belief or action at odds with the doctrine of the Roman Catholic Church

heretic (HER-uh-tik) *noun* a person whose actions or beliefs are considered to be heresy

Holy Roman Empire (HOH-lee ROH-muhn EM-pire) *noun* a Roman Catholic empire that stretched across much of central Europe from AD 973 to 1806

illegitimate (il-uh-JIT-uh-met) *adjective* born to a mother who is not legally married

martyr (MAR-tur) *noun* someone who is killed or made to suffer because of his or her beliefs

Mass (MASS) *noun* the main religious service in the Roman Catholic Church and some other churches

monastery (MON-uh-ster-ee) *noun* a group of buildings where monks live and work

noble (NOH-buhl) *noun* a person born into a wealthy family with the highest social rank in a society

Parliament (PAR-luh-muhnt) *noun* in England, the group of people who have been elected to make law

Protestant (PROT-uh-stuhnt) *noun* a Christian who does not belong to the Roman Catholic or Orthodox Church

Protestant Reformation (reh-for-MAY-shun) *noun* a 16th-century religious movement that aimed to change some practices of the Roman Catholic Church; it resulted in the establishment of Protestant churches in various European countries

psalm (SAHM) *noun* a sacred song or poem, especially one from the Book of Psalms in the Bible

ritual (RICH-oo-uhl) *noun* a set of actions that is always performed in the same way as part of a religious ceremony or social custom

rosary (ROH-zer-ee) *noun* a string of beads used by Roman Catholics in counting prayers

Roman Catholic Church (ROH-muhn KATH-uh-lik church) *noun* a Christian church that has the Pope as its leader

seizure (SEE-shur) *noun* a sudden attack of illness

succession (suhk-SESH-uhn) *noun* the order in which one person after another takes over a title or throne

theses (THEE-seez) *noun* ideas or arguments that are to be debated

treason (TREE-zuhn) *noun* the crime of betraying one's country by spying for another country or helping an enemy during a war

FIND OUT MORE

Here are some books and Web sites with more information about Mary Tudor and her times.

BOOKS

Blashfield, Jean F. **England (Enchantment of the World, Second Series)**. New York: Children's Press, 2006. (144 pages)
Describes the history, geography, and people of England.

Heard, Nigel. **Edward VI and Mary: A Mid-Tudor Crisis? (Access to History)**. London: Hodder Murray, 2000. (160 pages)
Discusses the political, religious, and social changes that occurred during the reigns of Edward VI and his sister Mary I.

McGurk, John. **The Tudor Monarchies, 1485-1603**. Cambridge, UK; New York: Cambridge University Press, 1999 (124 pages)
An overview of the Tudor monarchs, from Henry VII to Elizabeth I.

Slavicek, Louise Chipley. **Bloody Mary (History's Villains)**. Detroit: Blackbirch Press, 2005. (112 pages)
A biography of the queen who was determined to restore her kingdom to what she considered the one true religion.

WEB SITES

http://www.hrp.org.uk/
This site, Historic Royal Palaces, is an online tour of many of the famous buildings where Tudor history took place, such as Hampton Court and the Tower of London.

http://www.pbs.org/wnet/sixwives/index.html
PBS created this fun and informational companion site to its popular series The Six Wives of Henry VIII.

http://www.royal.gov.uk/output/Page1.asp
The official Web site of the British Monarchy provides a wealth of information on the history of the monarchy, including a profile of Mary Tudor.

http://www.tudorhistory.org/
This Web site, one of the most comprehensive sources of information on the Tudor family, includes chronologies, detailed biographies, and primary source materials.

For Grolier subscribers:
http://go.grolier.com/ **searches:** Mary I; Henry VIII; Catherine of Aragon; Anne Boleyn; Protestantism; Roman Catholic Church; Edward VI; Elizabeth I; Reformation; Martin Luther

INDEX

Author's Note and Bibliography

Mary Tudor is in many ways a tragic character. Born into royalty, she had little control over her life. She lived at the whim of her father. She was brought up in a strict Catholic household, and her faith was deeply ingrained from early childhood. It was what gave her strength in the years after her family fell apart.

The English people had mixed feelings about their queen. On the one hand, they loved her because she was her father's daughter and the rightful heir to the throne. Catholics in the realm hoped she would return their country to the "true faith." Protestants, at first just nervous, came to hate her.

As you read this book, try to put yourself in Mary's place. Think about the choices she faced as a queen and as a woman of the sixteenth century. Would you have made the same choices? Do her good intentions make her actions any less evil?

While Mary is not as well known as her famous father Henry VIII and her half sister Elizabeth, her reign is well documented.

The following works were the most helpful in writing this book:

Erickson, Carolly. **Bloody Mary, The Remarkable Life of Mary Tudor**. New York: Doubleday, 1978.

Loades, David. **Mary Tudor, A Life**. Cambridge, MA and Oxford, UK: Blackwell, 1989.

Loades, David. **Mary Tudor: The Tragical History of the First Queen of England**. Kew, Richmond, Surry, UK: The National Archives, 2006.

Manchester, William. **A World Lit Only by Fire, The Medieval Mind and the Renaissance, Portrait of an Age**. Boston: Little, Brown, 1992.

Marshall, Rosalind. **Mary I**. London: HMSO, 1993.

Weir, Alison. **The Children of Henry VIII**. New York: Ballantine, 1996.

—Jane Buchanan